Colours of Poetry
XIII

PLATITUDES OF MIND

by
Colin Michael

ISBN: 9798468169407
Imprint: Independently published
Colours of Poetry XII by Colin Michael 2021

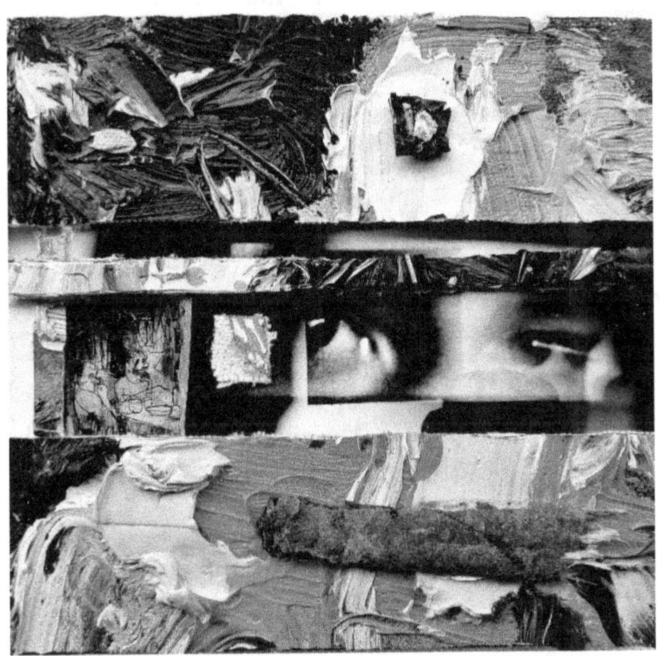

Cover and all Art by Colin Michael

Contents

Foreword

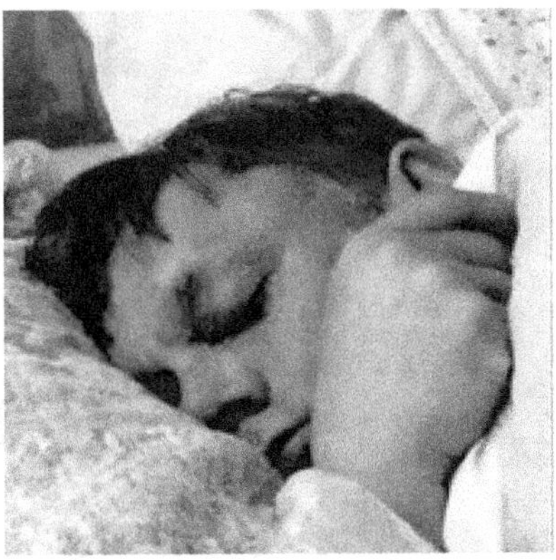

I don't wish to be pigeonholed. I know it helps to categorize into groups in order to come to some kind of rationality to my work. For me I dislike this as it could influence later writings (if I read any comments that is) and it would also narrow down my broad spectrum of trains of thoughts that flow freely through my mind. I have no agenda to change the world or people's minds just to feed a modicum of "let's see it a different way". This is why my poetry and prose are the way they are. If there is an unconscious thread it is "life" as I view it from all senses. It evolves.

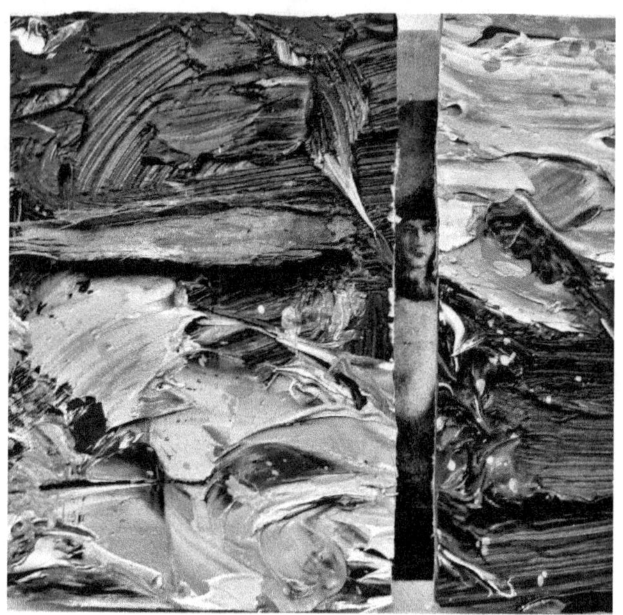

"Black and Blue"

366

Similar

I know you're all black and blue
Falling I felt the same as you

The pain that we felt inside
Only made us feel our love subside

Now that we say we're sorry
As we dry our tears of worry

I know I will never find another you
Even now I am black and blue.

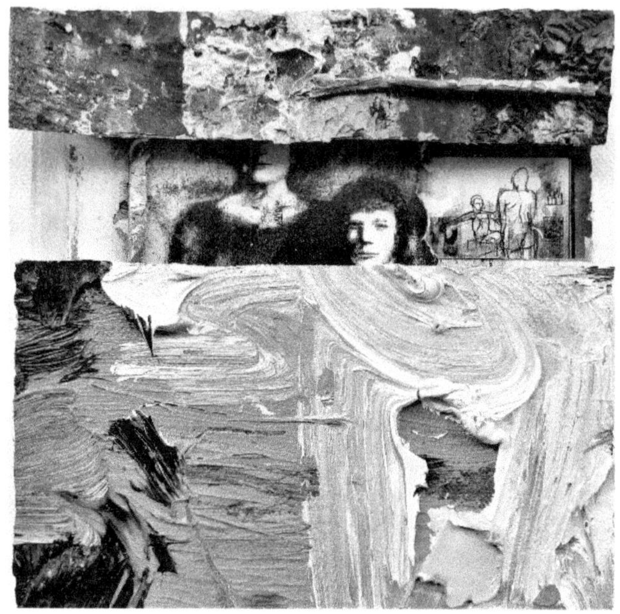

Everything is different

367

Just think

If you could think for a little while
That everything could be different

It wouldn't hurt in so many ways
I never meant to leave in such a way

Whether it could change things anyway
I could not take the pain you caused

Expecting me not to notice the changes
The two glasses the opened bottle of wine

You left on the kitchen table late last night
The secret diary you keep in your drawer

Was unlocked opened on the floor
It was time for me to go walk out that door

Everything is different difficult it's changed
I've turned my pages once more.

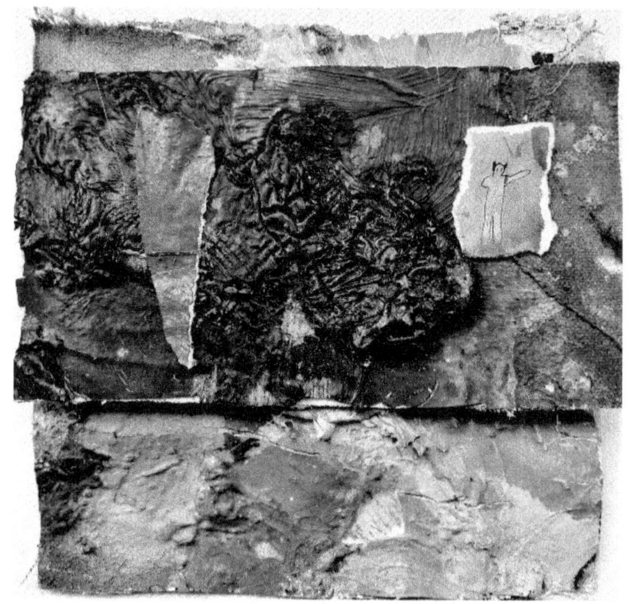

Hard to take

368

Probably

Truth is too hard to take
Thrusted upon your face
By the love of your life

When it's about you
Brutal honest truths
Disturb the inner core

It must be said
Every word spoken
It's one viewpoint

Probably?

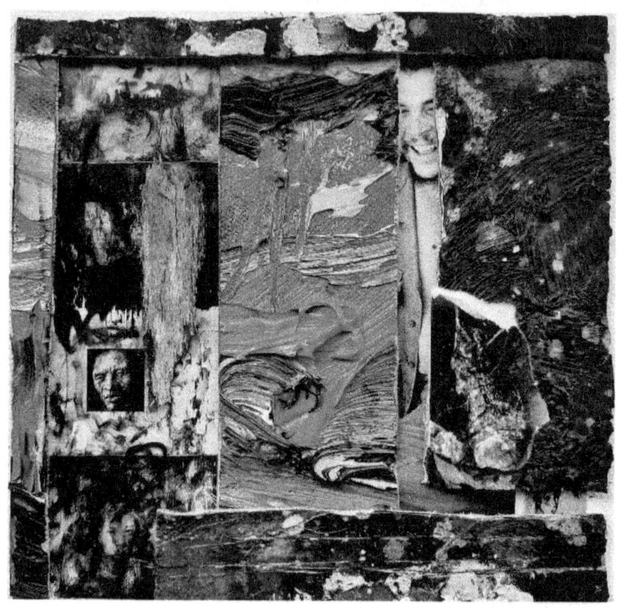

The vacancy in my glare

369

Way out

Paradise is only just around the corner
The man in the raincoat said dripping wet
Holding a bottle gesturing with his hand
Looking perplexed at the vacancy in my glare
Waving uncontrollably "that way stupid"
Moving the general direction he motioned
Joining the group of other confused souls
Could this be the right line to find paradise
Who knows as no one uttered a single word
Either side there were vague misty images
Unrecognizable or so it came across like that
Were they memories of past family members
Relations have only been spoken in faint whispers
We don't talk about what uncle John did
If this was the road to novena then forget it
Let's bailout at the next level marked way out.

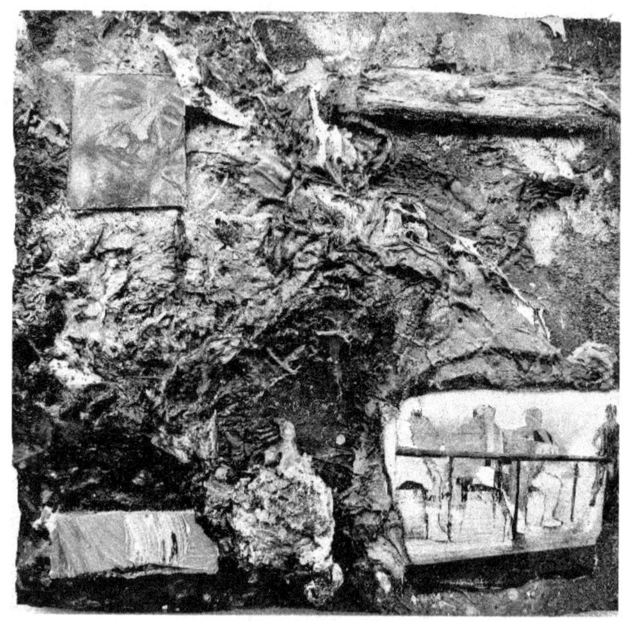

Depth of depravity

370

Good morning

The need to stand erect yet bent and tall
Not to yell to the scales that tilt

The imbalance in favour of others
Enveloping the sweet breath of maiden's

Who devoured every actionable desire?
Drawing upon a distressing depth of depravity

That mysterious inner fire of serenity
As morning weakens the ironman in you.

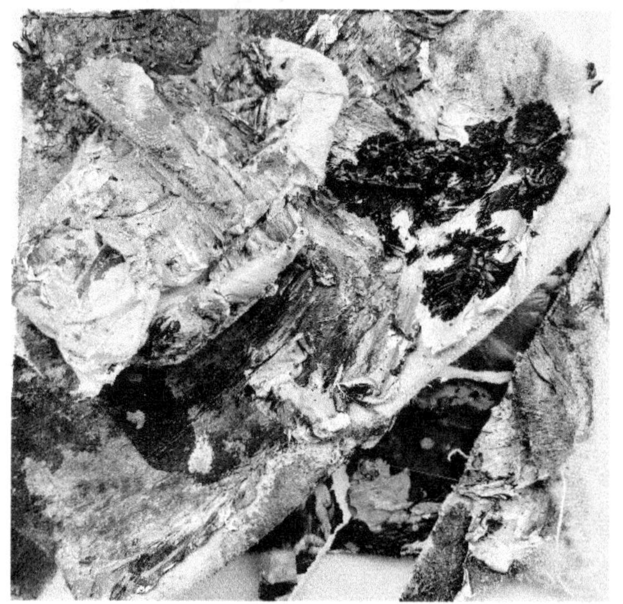

Feather light

371

Beacon of hope

White blossom falls lightly

As feather-light snowflakes

Caressing the light mooning breeze

Passing over the fields of spring

Gently cover the ground

With shades of white upon white

Silently caressing each other

Laying side by side

Softly whispering words of wisdom

A glimmer of hope over the horizon

Beckons the sunrises of warmth

Of a bounty of fruitfulness to come.

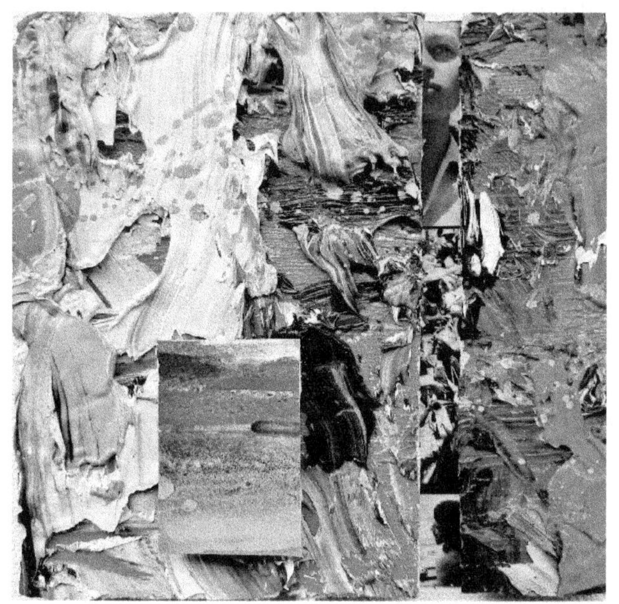

Crystal dew

372

Celebrate

It was a lovely spring morn'
With endless possibilities before

Trees dripping with crystal dew

Birds flitting from branch to branch
Chirping their signature songs

A clear yellow sun woke the day

Warming curled up sleepy leaves
Turning their selves to face the light

It was a day to celebrate life's life.

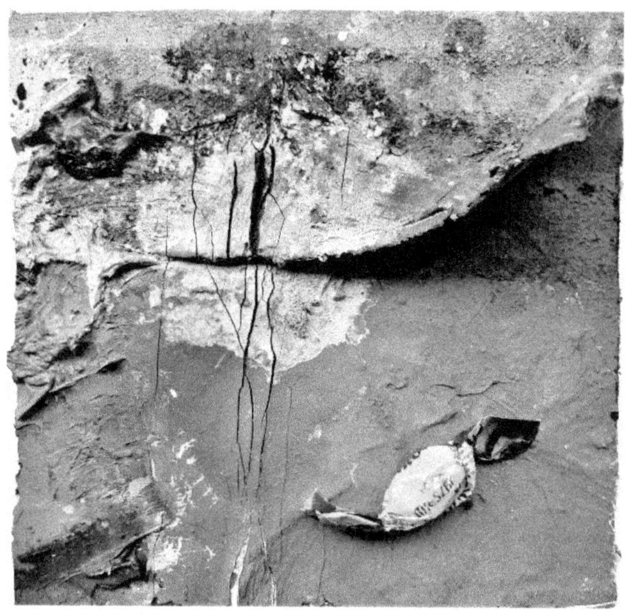

Pure white crystals

373

Solution

I wandered lonely as an acid cloud

Upon town, city scales and dales

Dripping tears to crave your mind

As the blades of windmills spin

Cover this green and pleasant land

Cutting lines of pure white crystals

Burning in the peace pipes of depravity

Driving deep into societies discord

As l wonder as a solution to no solution.

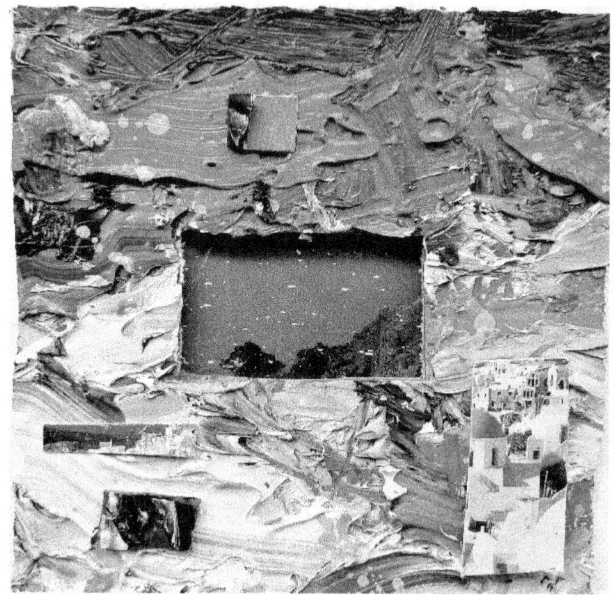

Outside the back door

374

Seven-year itch

An Email...

Subject: *"Hope you arrived safely Darling"*

"So you thought I did not know

About this so-called business trip

It was a ruse to have a romantic holiday

With your blonde bombshell secretary

Straight out of a reality show

Which is it now I forget how many

What, at least seven or is it seventeen?

All called Katakana from Georgia ex USSR

The one who calls in the middle of the night

Demanding an urgent signature at the office

Harry the locksmith has just arrived

I must be quick with my news from home

Your cat fluffy is outside the back door

In a sealed box for seven days now

The Charity shop have the Saville row suits

Church's shoes were given to a homeless man

The one you always give ten pence too

I put your other phone on the talking clock

Permanently locked with Australia

Your secret bank account is suspended

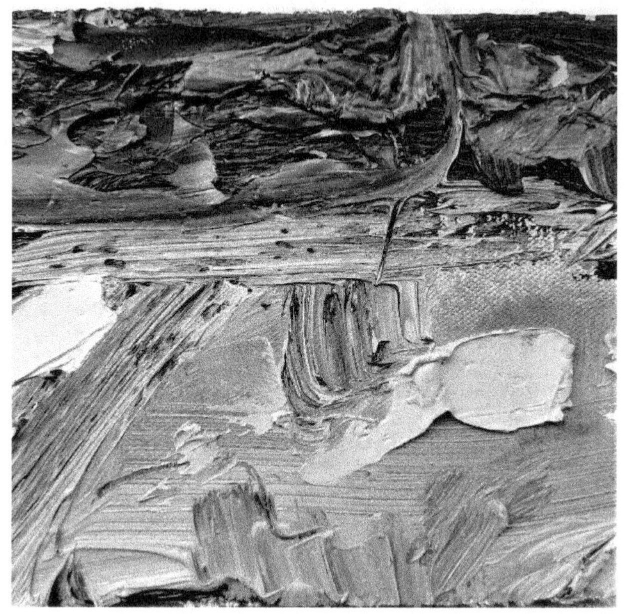

Mr White

Under the suspension of money laundering

Due to a transaction to Colombia a Mr. White

An anonymous letter sent to the bank

Your dear loving mother has been sectioned

Under the mental action of 1984

You filled a report of abuse as a minor

When you were on holiday in Wales in 1966

This was uncovered by a local journalist

You remember him Tommy the Nutter

The school friend you bullied

The company your work for has receipts

Of bought jewellery in Tiffany's New York

With a return trip on the last Concorde

Apart from the above minor things

I have filled a detailed police complaint

With photos of the bruises on my back

Enjoy your working trip to Barbados

Lots of love on your return to England

Faithful devoted wife of seven years"

Friday 13th June 2.27 am

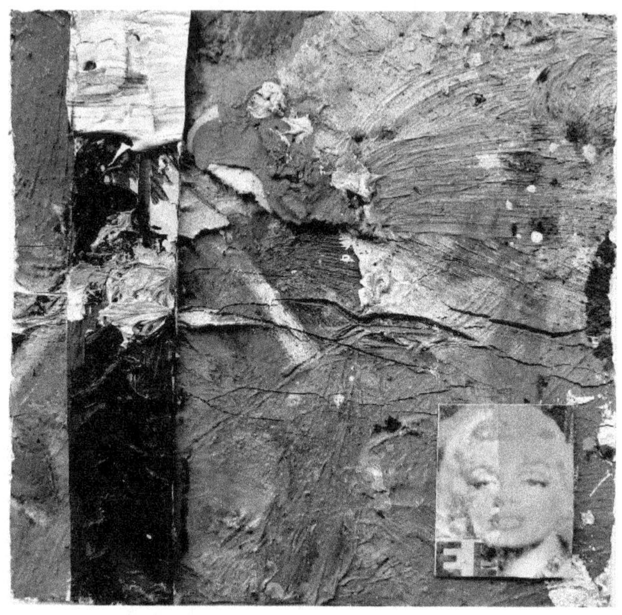

I'm in the middle

375

Approval

I haven't started

I'm in the middle
I'm at the end

Knowing when to begin
Knowing when to stop

It's never the solution
It's never the revolution

When it's approved
When it's possible

To start the circle
To stop the cycle

I haven't finished.

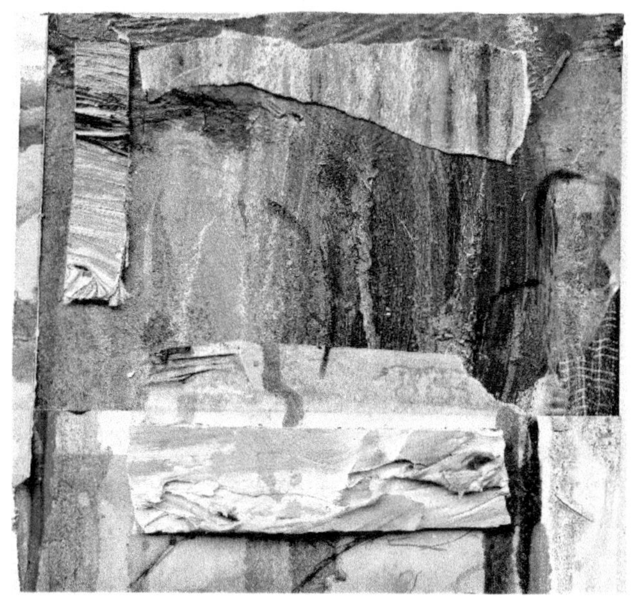

Leaving no trace

376

Broken

The window into your heart
Is likely been blown away

Opening a vacuous void
Your consolatory glare

Thinking you could save me
As your looks hide the truth

This wounded bleeding heart
Fear not as the cut runs deep

With no sense of forgiveness
The blade is resharpened

Plunged with surgical precision
Leaving no trace whatsoever

Walk away from this secret world
Of cold hearts and minds unbound

A sense of lustrous contempt
The window of opportunity closed.

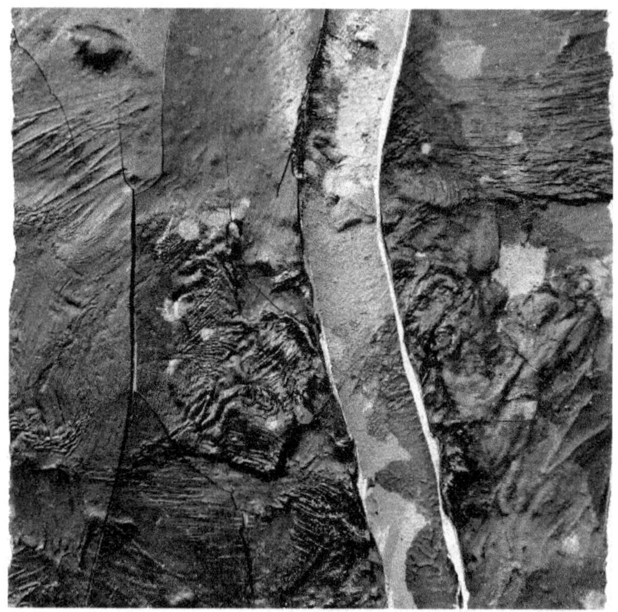

Share the experience

377

What a weekend

We waxed lyrically about virtual shadows

That boxed dancing lights of luminosity

Upon the walls that surrounded sounds

In stereophonic bouncing bubbles of joy

Floating over the clouds of heads of youths

While the underground new age purging

To the bass and drum of high fidelity

We are all as one with hands in the air

Popping pumping pulsating pleasure

Feeling the need to share the experience

A weekend of unbridled love for life.

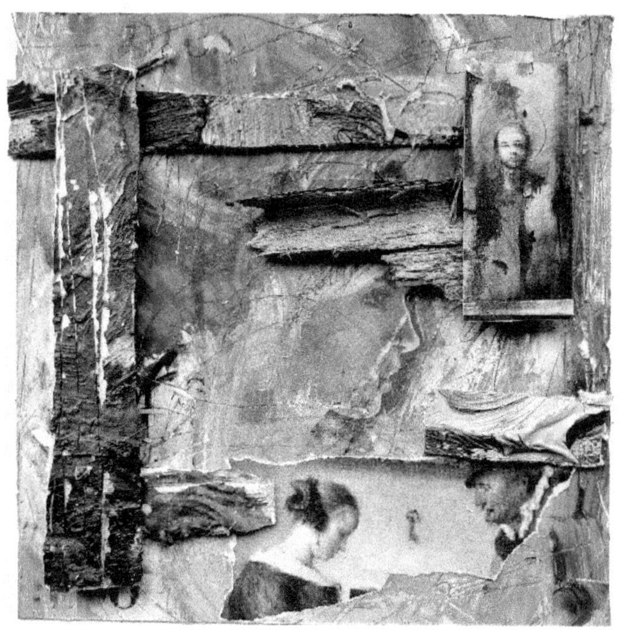

Most personal private thoughts

378

Better the devil

The devil sits on my shoulder
Picking incessantly at my mind

Causing no end of troubles
With impure thoughts of depravity

Burrowing into the cavity's solitude
That hold most personal private thoughts

Data mining that's what the man said
As he plugged me into his box of tricks

This won't hurt buttoning up his white coat
Taking two steps back behind a glass panel

Hold your breath for a brief moment
BANG BANG AND AGAIN BANG!

A flash of brilliant cardinal red with a hint of smoke
Just like a painting by Hieronymus Bosch I thought

After that, I don't remember anything
Do I remember who I am, I think so, do I?

Though I do feel so much better the devil said
Still sitting comfortably on my shoulder.

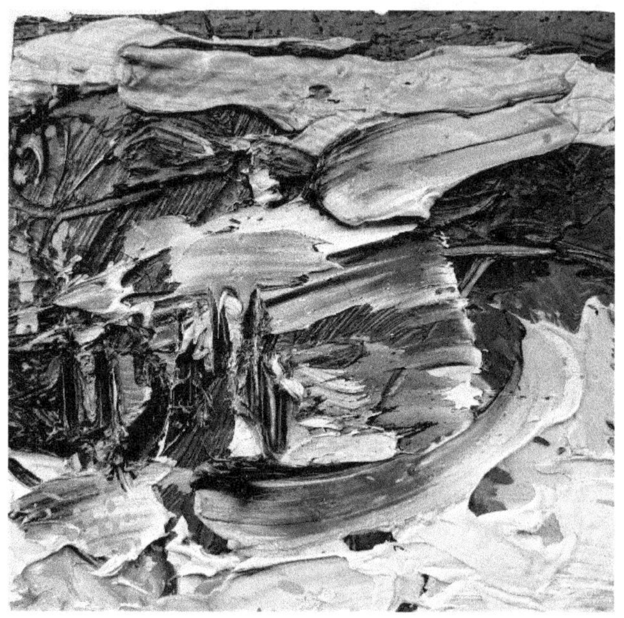

Winds whisper

379

Pagan platitude

Tribal heartlands of old
Oak trees that stand broad
Elders sit beneath as chieftains
Wisdom from the oracle at hand
Blue sky covers three-sixty degrees
Rich brown earth holds the answers
Winds whisper secret muttering
From generation to generation
Innocents go about their daily lives
Never questioning their being
Idyllic families share their days
What more could one ask for?

I know what...

More.

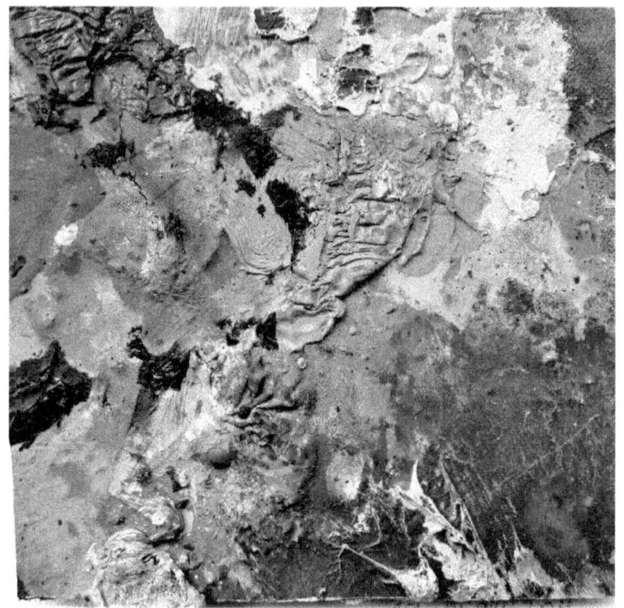

Can you describe it?

380

Off the wall

Wow!

What was that?

No idea

I think it was a "tangent"

It came out of nowhere

What was it like?

Off the wall

Not sure which

It slammed into me

What, just like that?

Yes! just like that

For no reason

Can you describe it?

No! its abstract.

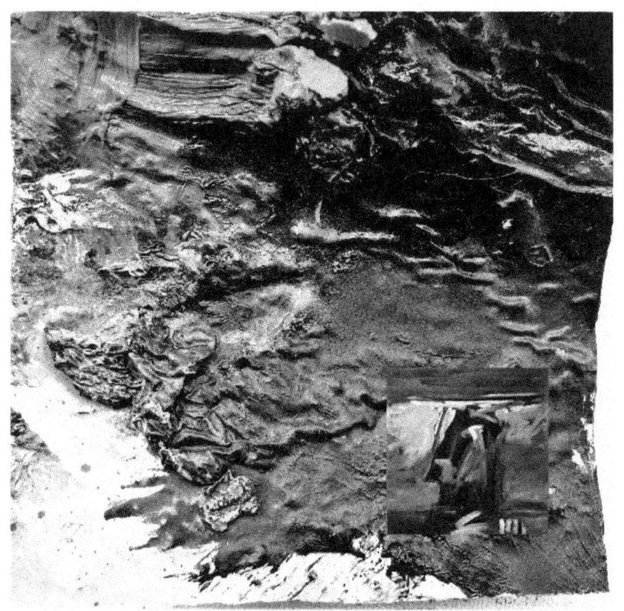

Evaluation is a matter

381

Portals

By the nature of it
It's going to change
Which is a good thing

According to Darwinian's
Evaluation is a matter
Of which this is a fact

One can debate this theory
But one can't dispute it
As day turns into night

After all who are we?
Mere mortals of matter
Lost in our own portals

Tripping over each other
On a daily basis
Not focusing on what is

Things are seen not heard
No one actually cares
Only but what's next to eat

Let's text Ubereats
I fancy a Chinese tonight
Well that's not going to last.

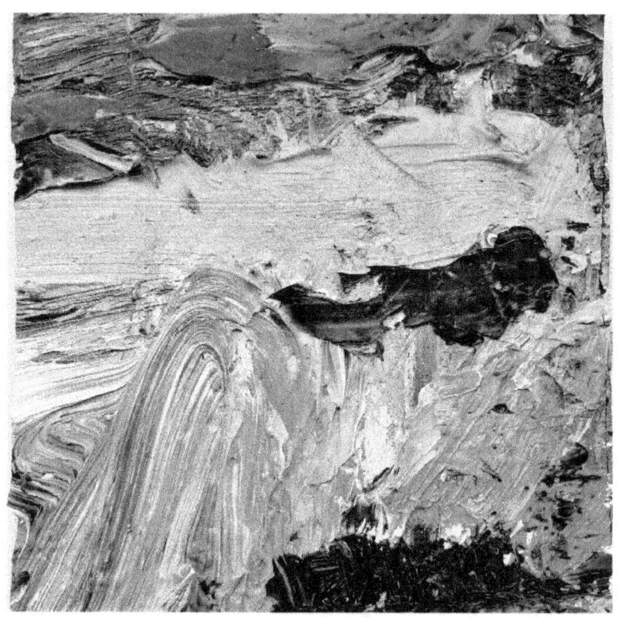

Still looking

382

Somewhere

It's a little too close
I don't want to mess up
Without you everything
Gets out of hand
Looking from the outside
Still looking in
I want to see it
Your way
Hoping it's not far
Though this could be
Out of reach
Letting this slip
Is not the way
I want to go.

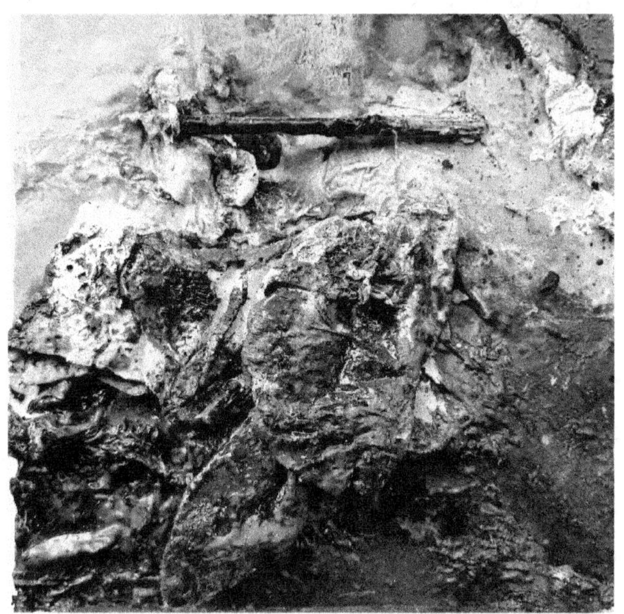

It's a pandemic

383

Nobody is listening

The phone lights up
With a buzz of concern
Hot breaking news
Flash up across
A laminated screen
What is next?
It's hot news
Fear the worse
It's a pandemic
Of epic proportion
This is nothing new
Nor hot off the press
It's more disturbing
Quietly pathetic
This media forensic
Of this creeping virus
Self-appointed unbiased reporters
Certified scientists of repute

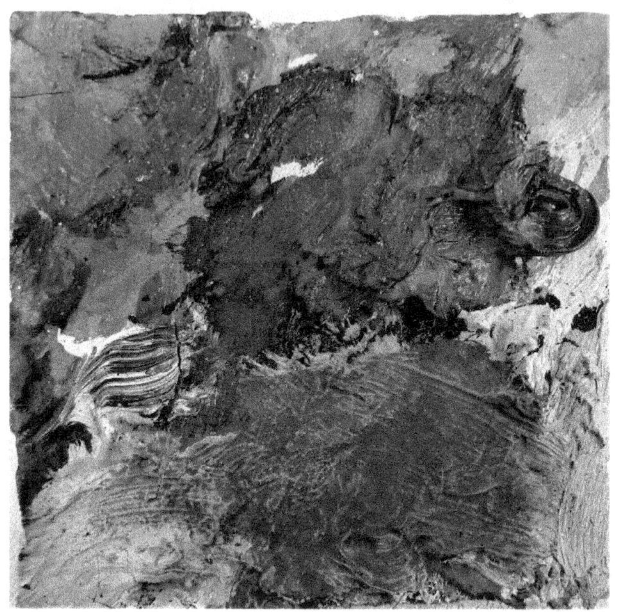

Misrepresentation of confusion

Search through data
Analyse scenarios
Of doomsday proportions
Paralysis of pandemic
Worldwide extinction
Out of control population
This constant rhetoric
We are all subjected to
There's a collective mistrust
About authorities realistic data
Results are disproportional
Misrepresentation of confusion

What do they believe?
Are we or not on the brink?
Let's all have a drink
Try not to think
It's overwhelming
As small-minded as we are
Well informed we are not
Reflect without respect
After all, is anyone listening
To us?
I don't think so
I know so.

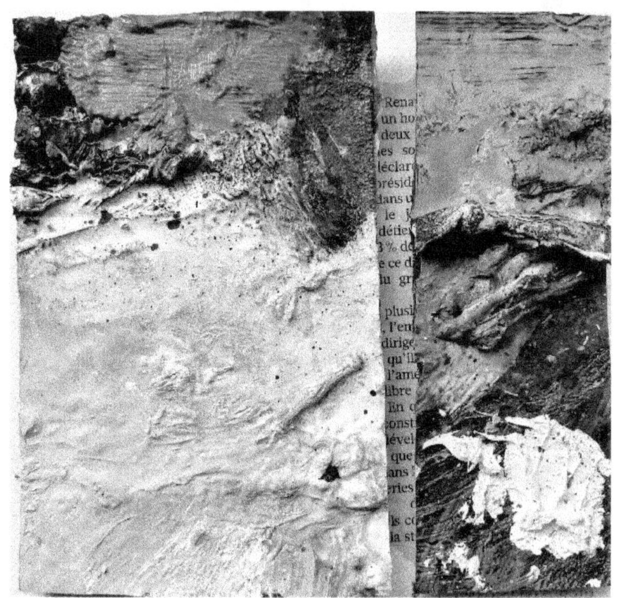

Half-closed eyes

384

Water bed

You can be so tired
That you can't go to sleep
With whispers in the head
All chit-chatting about you

With half-closed eyes
The body half paralyzed
Sounds muffled
Under a water bed

As a small bubble ascends
Collecting as one
Stuck at the top
There is no escape

I just want to go to sleep
Anxieties all but done
Slowly the hands on the clock
Tick tick away till dawn.

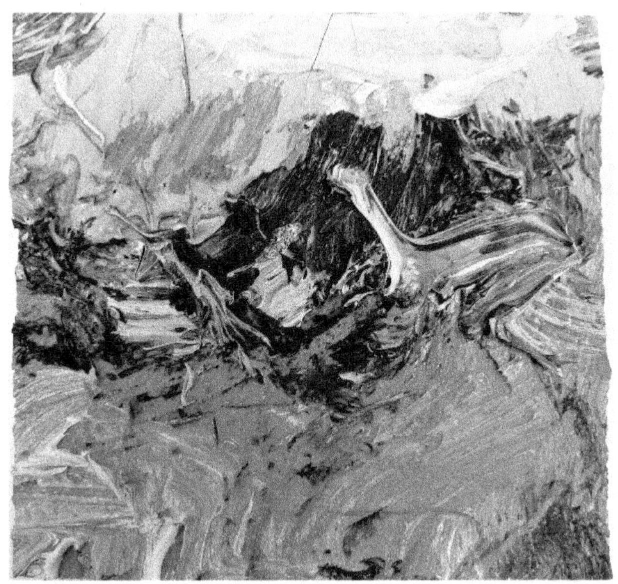

What was wrong?

385

Nothing was said

I spoke too soon it was 1969
I stood naked in the playground
Everyone was staring at me
Laughing their heads off
Pointing at my "Netherlands"
What was wrong?
As I glance downstairs
I was on fire
All hell had broken loose
The elephant was not in the room
He was out trumpeting
For all to see
I had no control
This monster was on the rampage
The bedroom door opened abruptly
Here's a nice cup of hot tea dearly
Now get dressed
We don't want to miss the school bus
Do we darling?
Mother disappear downstairs
Nothing was said...

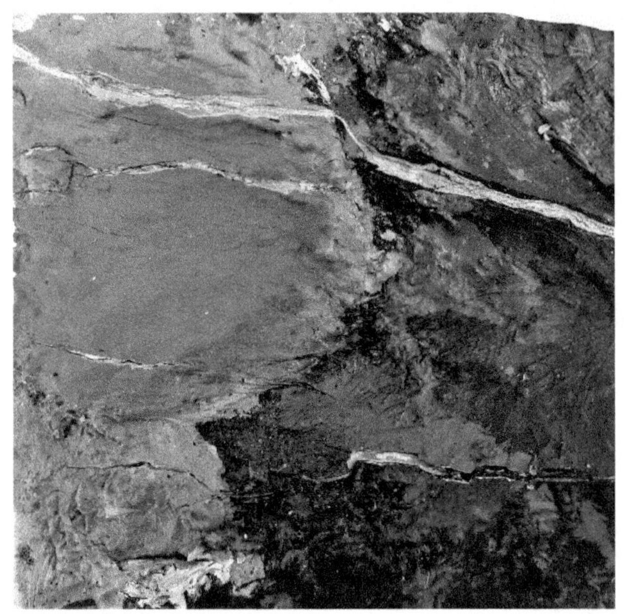

Children played

386

Magnolia revisited

Under the sweet smell of the magnolia tree
Sophie lay reading the latest hot gossip
Elle magazine was the comic of choice

Around the children played in the pool
Shouting splashing doing what young do best
Annoying the adults with their grown-up stiffness

Margo hardly lifted a hand to ask for more wine
Though the servant noticed that a finger did move

Father by this time was sucked annoyingly on his
Havana
Sweetly rolled wrapped round on a thigh of Cuban maid

Intensely he was scripting the evening's events
Old school with a fountain pen squirting blobs of ink
All in the wrong places like spider footprints

A family play was being transcribed word for word
No doubt it would be a Greek tragedy of epic
importance

The family wandered on with the warmth of summer.

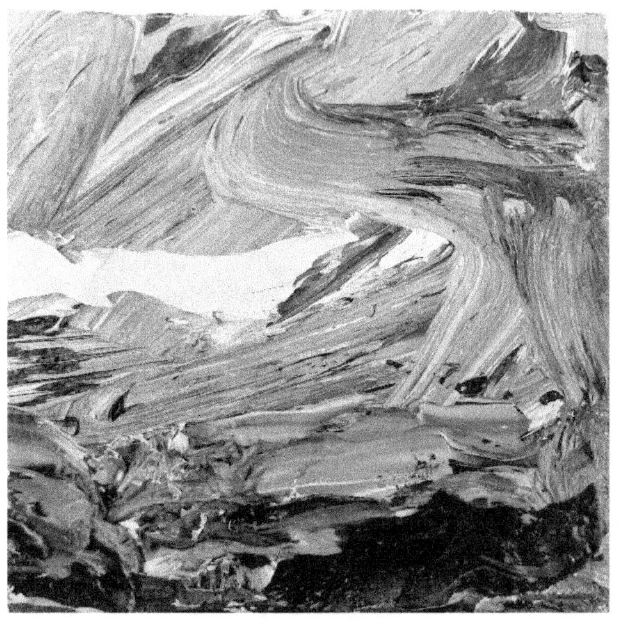

Does it end

387

Junctions

Life is a road map
What's that about?
Is it an A to Z
To where to go
With junctions
Do you get off
Or go round?
Does it end
At a cliff edge
Or continue on and on?
Is there a fast lane
A slow lane?
Are there run-off areas
For safety reasons?
I bought mine
At a stationary
Overpriced of course
Captive audience
It was out of date
The back cover said
Correct as time of printing
Nineteen eighty-four
What does that mean?
Things will change
For better or worse
Who knows after all?
It's a road map for life
And is north true north?
What's that about?

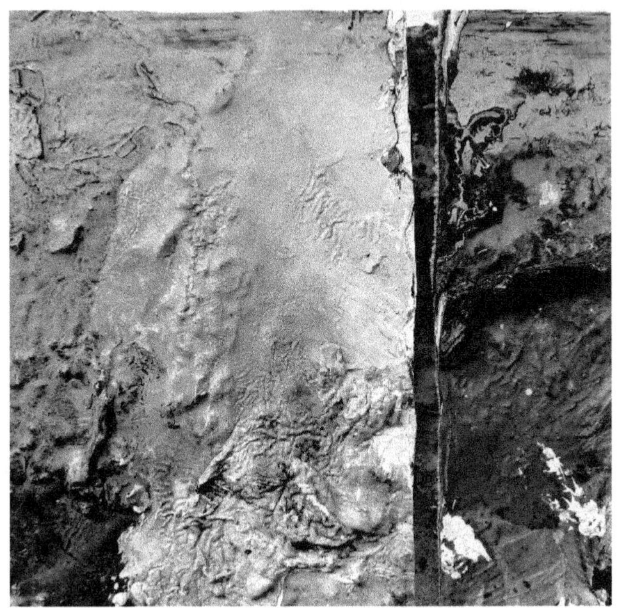

It's not going down

388

On paper

Honestly, this looked good on paper

Ok in my imaginary paper head
Then I wrote it down it sucked
I felt I was chasing words around a table
With legs that kind of go all the way
To the top and never stop

Ok long legs I have a thing for
No, I don't I just made that bit up
To get my mind off the fact that
I was writing this poem or I thought so

Ok it's not going down on paper that well
After all, I scrunched it up into a neat ball
Kicking it to the bin across the room
You know the one that saves the planet
By making it into loo rolls or something
You know the ones that looks grey
Friends say it scratches their butt

Ok no they don't to your face
They do have a strange face after a visit
Is it my cooking that is so hot as in cool
I'm getting off target here or is it offline
That reminds me I must call the doctor
I need to see him about that rash
The one caused by the paper I use

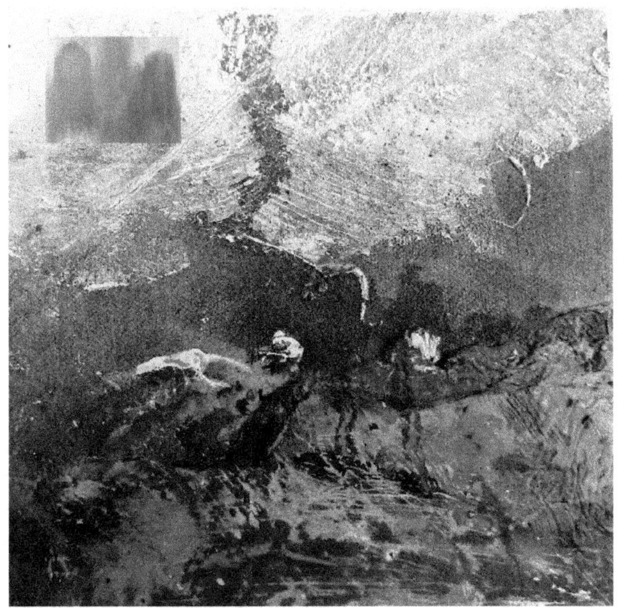

From the edge

389

One digit away

It's too complicated
This four-digit code
Well for me that is

I typed it in
Multiple times
Each time rejected

Is my birth date wrong
Was I born too late
I can't relate

This situation
Compounded by illogic
Are we just a number

Just a figment
Of a Digitised selfie
Images black dots

Are we what we are
Nothing at all
One number away

From the edge
Leaning over
Looking down

Two barrels
Of a black hole
Into the abyss.

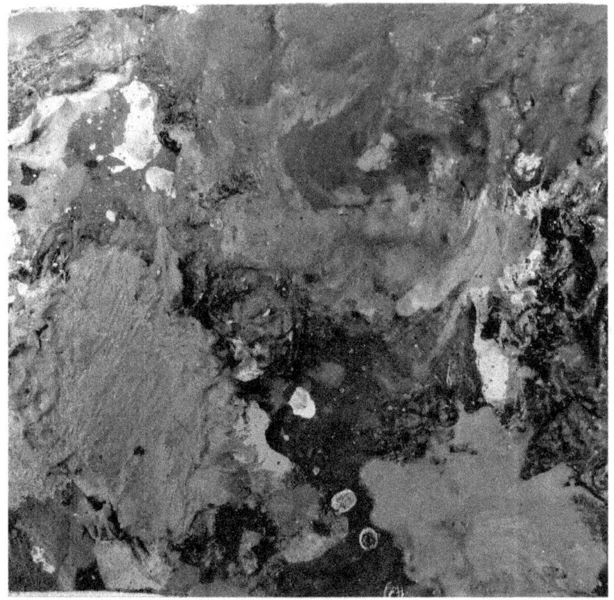

When you need to cry alone

390

Do you go

You can cry all day
In your own space

No one can see you
Hiding in your place

Away from judging
Eyes of confusion

It's time to reflect
Situations to contemplate

Viewpoints compounded
Anything could happen

And it usually does
Just when it shouldn't

Where to go I have no idea
When you need to cry alone.

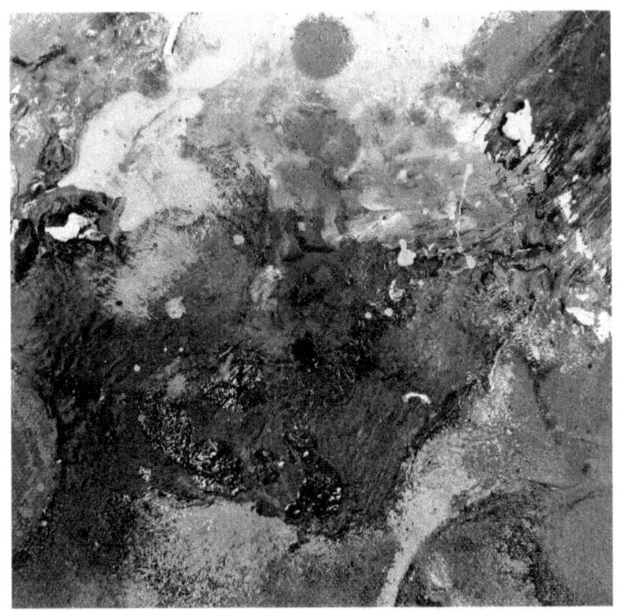

I have issues

391

It's over

Do you think too much
Hopefully not
As it hurts physically

Like hail hitting your head
While standing in the road
Waiting for the bus

The one that hasn't arrived
Come on how hard is it
You get designated lines

We are mere mortals don't we
Plus you pull away
Every time someone runs
Waving mouthing "wait
Please don't go Please"

I'm going to the doctors
I have issues
That need immediate action

Plus you're earlier this time
What is that about
I am overthinking this scenario

Relax let's sit down
Have a nice cup of tea
Wait which tea to have

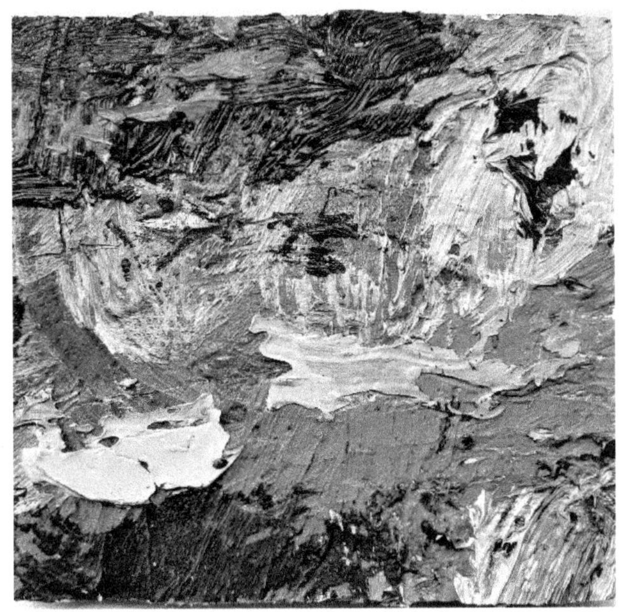

Boston Harbour

It's important
I mean really

Breakfast tea, Oolong,
Morning tea, Darjeeling
Afternoon tea, Earl Grey

It's not just any old tea
Britain built an empire on tea
Then the Americans dumped it
In Boston Harbour.

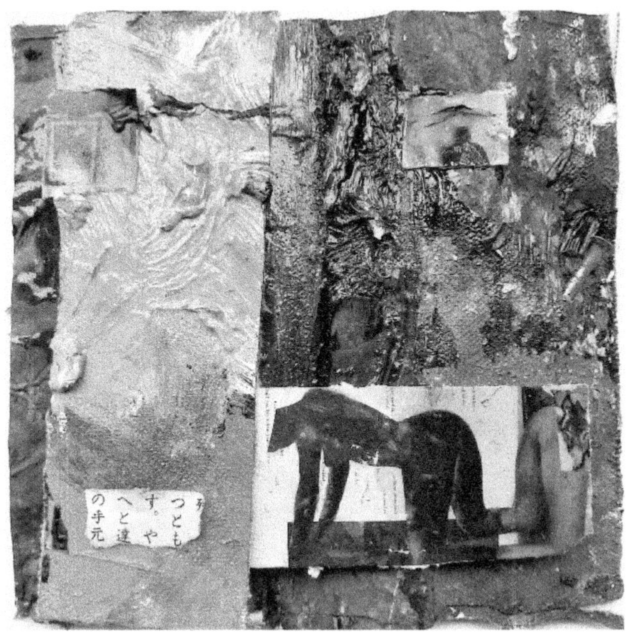

A void without

392

Quiet poof

Are you happy

When the world ends
It will be with a bang they say

Me myself and my mates think not
It will be with a crying whimper

As sort of quiet poof
Like a half-hearted cough

The one you try to get out
Though lodged annoyingly in the throat

What will be left is nothing
A void without even a black hole

Is it going to be sad
No idea as we are all gone

So why worry
It's over it's done and dusted

I thought there would be nothing
Now you say there is dust

Come on leaving it out
Ok maybe a bit of space dust

Happy now?

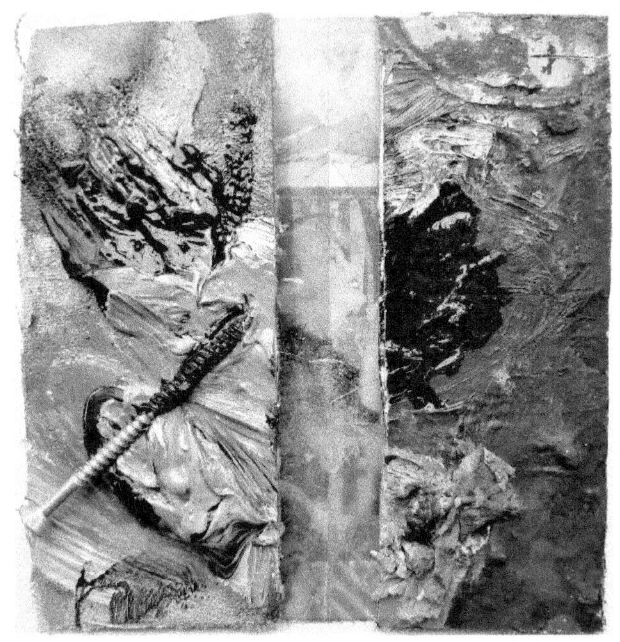

Space to see

393

Space 22

I look up to the stars
To see Richard Branson

Passing over in a flash
What an amazing feat

To have floating feet
So high above our heads

With ours grounded instead
Like so many I will wish

To go up in space to see
What this pioneer saw

Now due to his hard work
The answer is clearly yes

We can go into space
And experience floating feet.

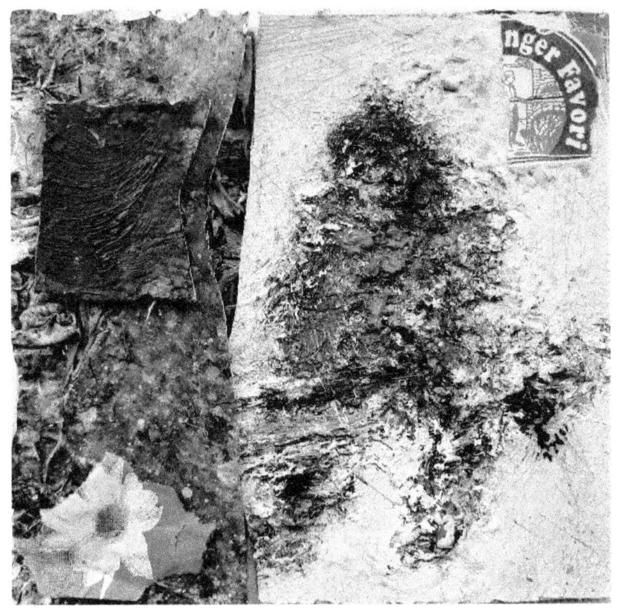

Don't give up

394

Shame

I keep trying
Keep dying
For your love

When are you
Going to show
Me your love

It's crying shame
There's no one
But me to blame

It's so easy
Don't give up
On me just yet

I just want
Your love
For heaven's sake.

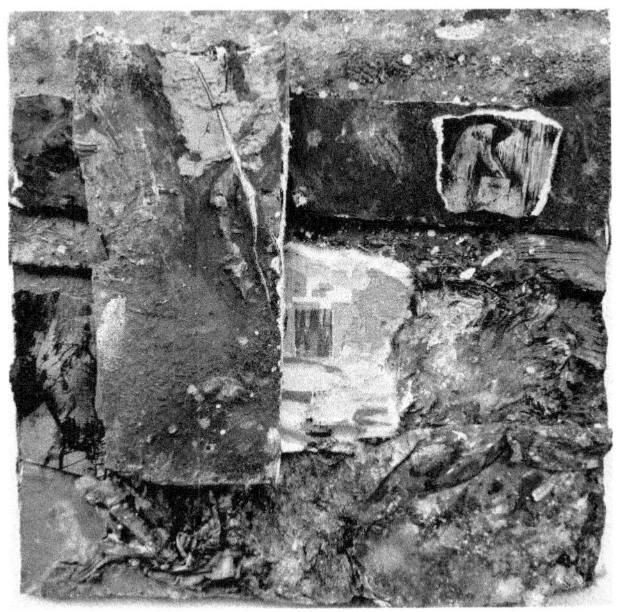

Somewhere inside

395

Red hot chili

It's a frigging pain in the arse

My laptop has a mind of its own

Turning itself on and off

Not responding to my commands

What's that about I asked myself

Mr Micro Soft "ware" are you now?

Somewhere inside eating my chips

Your red-hot chili flavour sucks

As my mouse finger burnt to a crisp

Trying to respond, "Damn you, respond!".

Biography

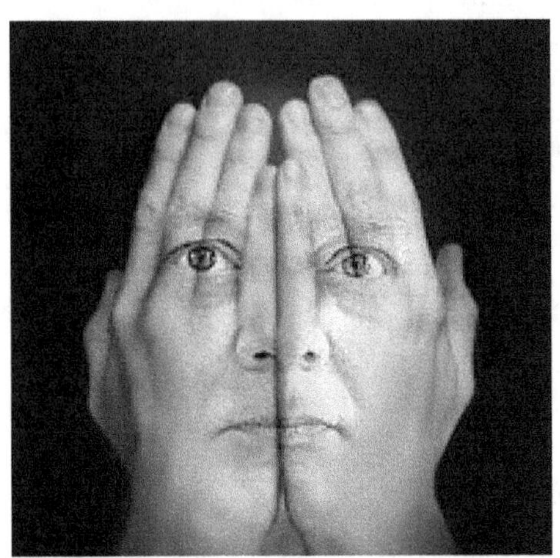

Colin Michael
Artist, Poet, YouTube Video maker

Born in Bulawayo in 1959.
Lived in Salisbury (Harare), Southern Rhodesia
(Zimbabwe) 1959-66
Emigrated to London, England in 1966
Emigrated to Paris, France in 2018

Education.
Alfred Beit, Mabelreign, Southern Rhodesia (Zimbabwe)
Middleton Rose Hill, Sutton, London
Boughton Monchelsea Maidstone Kent
Biggin Hill, Bromley, Kent
Churchill, Westerham, Kent
Ravensbourne Art College, London
Slade School of Art, London

Awards.
D&AD Gold
Evening Standard, Best Advertisements
Paperchase, best Brochure
Best Painting, National Society of Painters Sculptors &
Printmakers
The London Group, Best New Artist selected by Albert
Irvin RA

Solo and Group Exhibitions.
1987 to present day - London and Paris.

Associations, past and present.
Treasurer, Hon' Member National Society of Painters
Sculptors & Printmakers.
The Arts Club, May Fair, London
Who's Who in Art
Beckenham Heritage Group (BHG) Famous People

Currently living and working in Paris.

Other Books Published on Amazon
Colours of Poetry, Number One.
17.12.2017
Colours of Poetry II, Painting with words.
10.03.2020
Colours of Poetry III, No Rhythm nor reason.
20.04.2020
Tea & Poetry. The first 100 works from 'Colours of poetry'.
06.05.2020
Colours of Poetry IV, Pros and cons.
22.05.2020
Colours of Poetry V, Paradoxically, seeking.
20.06.2020
Colours of Poetry VI, Ambiguous parodies.
31.10.2020
Coffee & Poetry, The second 100 works from 'Colours of Poetry'.
24.12.20
Colours of Poetry VII, And then some.
01.01.2020
Colours of Poetry VIII, Affairs of the written word.
12.01,21
Colours of Poetry IX, Contemplate the now.
31.01.2021
Colours of Poetry X, Literary Intervention.
23.02.2021
Wine & Poetry. The third 100 works from 'Colours of poetry'.
06.02.2021

Colours of Poetry X1, Violence with disparity.
28.08.2021
Colours of Poetry XII. Is it black and white
30.08.2021

www.ingramcontent.com/pod-product-compliance
Lightning Source LLC
Chambersburg PA
CBHW070918160726
48004CB00003B/1422